VICKY NGUYEN - A MEMOIR OF HEROISM AND HUMOR

From the Tales of the Boat Baby Experience to the Heights of Greatness

Billy Jones

VICKY NGUYEN - A MEMOIR OF HEROISM AND HUMOR

Copyright © 2025 by **Billy Jones**

ALL RIGHTS RESERVED

No part of this book may be reproduced, distributed, or transmitted in any form or by any means without the prior written permission of the publisher, except in the case of brief quotations embodied in critical reviews and certain other noncommercial uses permitted by copyright law.

ISBN: 978-1-300-38944-6

To Vicky Nguyen, whose unwavering strength, resilience, and dedication have shaped an inspiring journey of triumph. To every immigrant and refugee who has faced unimaginable challenges, yet continues to rise with hope and purpose. May this story honor your legacy and ignite the power of your own voice.

This book is for all who believe in the possibility of transformation and the power of perseverance.

CONTENTS

Introduction vi

Saigon's Last Breath – A Family on the Run 1

Pirates, Prayers, and the Sea that Wouldn't Swallow Us 6

The Refugee Camp Diaries 11

From Tent to Texas 17

Pho, Full House, and Fitting In 22

Growing Up with Grit – Education, Expectations & Extra Rice
.... 27

The Rise of a Voice 32

NBC, National Spotlight & Never Forgetting Home 37

Humor in Hardship 42

From Boat Baby to Boss Lady 46

Lessons from the Ocean 51

    Strength: The Ability to Endure and Overcome 51
    Humility: The Importance of Staying Grounded 52
    Faith: The Compass That Guided Her 53
    Gratitude: Recognizing the Gifts Along the Way 54
    Advice for Immigrants and Children of Refugees 55

Full Circle – Returning to Vietnam 56

    The First Steps on Home Soil 57
    Reconciliation with the Past 58
    Honoring Her Roots 59
    Healing and Moving Forward 60

Full Circle – Returning to Vietnam 61

    Encouraging the Youth 62
    Fighting Stereotypes and Challenging Misconceptions 63
    Celebrating Immigrant Stories 64
    Legacy in Motion 65

INTRODUCTION

Vicky Nguyen's story doesn't begin in a cradle, nor in a comfortable hospital room. It begins on the open sea—a place where survival was a gamble, and hope was the only compass. Born in the wake of war, amid the chaos of Vietnam's collapse, Vicky was part of a generation known not just by name or nationality, but by circumstance. She was a "boat baby," one of thousands of children carried to freedom by the courage of their parents, across waters that swallowed dreams as easily as they carried them.

To understand Vicky Nguyen is to understand that legacy. It's not just about her success as a national investigative journalist or her rise to prominence as a trusted voice in American media. It's about the storm she was born into—one that wasn't of her own making—and the sunlight she chose to seek with every step she took afterward. The story of Vicky is the story of a survivor, a daughter of resilience, and a woman whose humor is as sharp as her insight.

Her parents, like so many others after the fall of Saigon in April 1975, faced a decision no one should ever have to make: stay in a collapsing country under Communist control or risk everything for a chance at freedom. They chose the latter. With little more than the clothes on their backs, they joined the waves of Vietnamese refugees who set out on rickety boats, unprotected against pirates, storms, starvation, and despair. Among them was Vicky's pregnant mother, carrying not only a child but also the weight of uncertainty.

That journey through the South China Sea was not romantic. It wasn't a sweeping movie scene of bravery and victory. It was raw, terrifying, and often degrading. Refugee boats were attacked by pirates, children died of dehydration, and families watched helplessly as loved ones slipped beneath the waves. But those who survived—like Vicky's family—emerged from the water marked not just by trauma, but by extraordinary strength.

Vicky Nguyen was born shortly after her family reached safety, in a refugee camp in Malaysia. Her arrival symbolized more than just the continuation of a bloodline—it represented hope. She was proof that life continues even in the most uncertain of places. She was, quite literally, born between worlds: a Vietnamese child destined to grow up American, shaped by both identities but not fully belonging to either. That tension—between homeland and new land, between survival and success—would define her worldview.

When her family arrived in the United States, the war was behind them, but the struggle was not. Like many refugees, her parents had to start over completely. Her father worked labor jobs. Her mother juggled roles as caregiver, homemaker, and part-time worker. They didn't speak English, didn't understand American customs, and didn't ask for sympathy. They asked only for a chance. Vicky grew up in that environment, a child who learned early how to translate not just words but cultures. She straddled the Vietnamese values of discipline and respect with the American ideals of individuality and freedom.

In her earliest memories, Vicky was already learning how to be the bridge between two worlds. She translated for her parents at grocery stores and doctor's offices. She helped them navigate the mail, the bills, and eventually the bureaucracy of the American Dream. But even then, humor found a place in her story. She recalls learning English from sitcoms like "Full House" and "Family Matters," often mimicking the exaggerated expressions and catchphrases she didn't yet understand. It was funny, but it was survival. Comedy, for Vicky, was never just entertainment—it was a coping tool.

The story of a "boat baby" is often told with heavy tones: tragedy, trauma, hardship. And yes, Vicky's life includes all those elements. But what sets her apart is how she chose to respond to them. From an early age, she decided that survival wasn't enough. She wanted to thrive. She didn't just want to tell stories—she wanted to uncover truth, hold power accountable, and speak for those whose voices were still silenced by the storms they had weathered.

As Vicky grew, so did her curiosity. She became a stellar student, driven not only by ambition but also by a desire to honor her parents' sacrifice. Her family didn't come to America for her to be comfortable; they came for her to have opportunity. That awareness never left her. It shaped her worldview, grounded her reporting, and gave her an empathy that shines through her work.

But despite the pressure, or perhaps because of it, Vicky always found space for laughter. Whether it was joking about the unique smell of fish sauce wafting from her childhood lunchbox or telling self-deprecating stories about cultural misunderstandings at school, she embraced humor as a means of connection. In classrooms where she was the only Asian face, she learned that a good joke could disarm cruelty. That laughter could build bridges faster than explanation.

Her identity as a Vietnamese-American was never simple. It came with internal conflict: wanting to fit in while honoring where she came from. Wanting to speak perfect English while preserving her family's language. Wanting to succeed by American standards while maintaining Vietnamese humility. But Vicky never shied away from the complexity. She leaned into it. She turned her in-between-ness into her superpower.

When she eventually stepped into journalism, it was with the same sense of mission that brought her parents across the sea. She wasn't just there to report—she was there to represent. To bring nuance to headlines. To highlight stories often overlooked. And to do it all while remaining deeply human: witty, sharp, and unafraid to laugh, even when the world felt heavy.

This memoir begins with a storm—not just the literal one that tossed boats on the South China Sea, but the emotional storm of leaving everything behind. And it leads us through a journey toward sunshine—not perfection, but purpose. Vicky's story is not just about escape or survival. It's about transformation. It's about becoming someone who doesn't forget the past but doesn't let it limit the future either.

The "boat baby" legacy is one of hardship, yes. But it's also one of astonishing grit. Of families who crossed oceans so their children could cross stages. Of women like Vicky Nguyen who rose from the margins and claimed their seat at the table—not by erasing their roots, but by honoring them. She represents the promise that even in chaos, new beginnings are possible. That even when you're born in a storm, you can still live in the sunshine.

As you turn the pages of this memoir, you'll laugh, you'll cry, and you'll understand why Vicky Nguyen's story isn't just hers—it belongs to every child of immigrants, every voice that's ever felt overlooked, and every reader who believes that the journey matters just as much as the destination.

CHAPTER 1

SAIGON'S LAST BREATH – A FAMILY ON THE RUN

In the final days of April 1975, the city of Saigon inhaled deeply, holding its breath in fear, anxiety, and unspoken grief. Then, with the roar of tanks and the crackle of distant gunfire, it exhaled in collapse. The war that had ravaged Vietnam for decades came to a harrowing end—not with peace, but with surrender. North Vietnamese troops breached the gates of the presidential palace, and the South Vietnamese flag was lowered for the last time. It was the fall of Saigon, and it marked not only the end of a nation, but the beginning of one of the greatest humanitarian crises of the twentieth century.

Among the tens of thousands who watched their homeland crumble was the Nguyen family—Vicky's family. Her parents, like so many others, were faced with a choice no one should ever have to make: remain under the threat of a regime they did not trust, or flee into the unknown, risking everything for the mere possibility of freedom. It was a decision made in the tension of chaos, fear, and love. It was also a decision that would come to define their legacy.

Vicky's mother, pregnant at the time, and her father, resourceful and quietly brave, were young and uncertain of the future. Yet they understood something fundamental: staying meant surrendering their dreams, their dignity, and perhaps even their lives. Fleeing meant hope, however slim. Hope for their unborn child. Hope for a life beyond Communism. Hope for a second chance.

The days leading up to their escape were shrouded in secrecy. Rumors swirled throughout the city like wildfire. American soldiers were evacuating, families were disappearing overnight, and the once-bustling streets of Saigon grew more desperate by the hour. Every loud noise could have been a gunshot. Every moment was a gamble.

Her father knew someone—someone who knew someone else—with access to a boat. That fragile thread of connection was their only chance. The escape would not be organized or orderly. It would be frantic, under the cover of darkness, with a thousand uncertainties and one overwhelming truth: there was no going back.

They left behind everything. Their home, their photographs, their possessions, and even some relatives they could not reach in time. There was no time to say proper goodbyes. No time for ceremony. Only time for escape. With just the clothes on their backs and the determination of people who had run out of options, they made their way to the docks, hiding among crowds, dodging checkpoints, hearts pounding with every step.

The boat itself was no luxury liner. It was barely seaworthy, overcrowded with other desperate souls—children clinging to mothers, elders whispering prayers, and men scanning the horizon for signs of rescue or danger. There was no space, no privacy, and no guarantee they would live to see another day. The South China Sea, infamous for its unpredictable storms and pirates, lay ahead.

During the voyage, they battled hunger, dehydration, and the agony of uncertainty. Pirates attacked at least once, threatening to rob and violate the already fragile group. Every day at sea was a negotiation with death. And yet, every day was also a testament to human resilience. Somehow, they endured.

In the middle of that survival, in a Malaysian refugee camp where the stench of overcrowding mingled with the smell of hope, Vicky's mother gave birth. It wasn't in a clean hospital. There were no sterile tools or caring nurses. Only the resilience of women who had carried generations on their backs, and the unwavering belief that the child they were welcoming into the world deserved better. That child was Vicky Nguyen.

She was born not in Vietnam and not yet in America, but somewhere in between. A child of liminality. A daughter of the sea. A survivor before she ever took her first breath.

The refugee camp where they waited was not a home, but a purgatory. The conditions were rough. Food was scarce. Disease was rampant. And yet, people helped each other. They shared what little they had. They told stories to distract their children from hunger. They laughed—yes, even laughed—because laughter was the only way to hold on to their humanity in the face of such loss.

Eventually, through a combination of luck, perseverance, and sponsorship, the Nguyen family was granted passage to the United States. They arrived in a land they had never seen, whose language they didn't speak, whose culture was alien, and whose people often looked at them with suspicion or pity. But they arrived as survivors. And more than that, as builders of a new legacy.

In those early days, her parents did everything they could to put food on the table. Her father took menial labor jobs, often working long hours for meager pay. Her mother learned to navigate this strange world with a baby on her hip and an iron will. They took ESL classes at night, scraped together money to buy a used car, and leaned on fellow Vietnamese refugees who had also made it across.

They rarely spoke about what they had lost. That was the unspoken rule among many first-generation immigrants—silence was survival. The pain, the fear, the grief—they were buried under the routines of work and responsibility. But they did tell one story, again and again: the story of how they got out. Of how, in the darkest night of Saigon's last breath, they found a way to escape.

That story became a lodestar for Vicky. As she grew up, she didn't just learn her ABCs or how to tie her shoes. She learned grit from her father's calloused hands. She learned sacrifice from her mother's quiet strength. And she learned the importance of voice—of having one, and using it—from the silence they carried.

When she later became a journalist, investigating some of the toughest stories in America, she often thought back to that escape. To the boat, to the storm, to the way her family refused to let fear define them. Her ability to ask hard questions, to pursue the truth, and to amplify voices that were ignored—those traits were not learned in a newsroom. They were inherited.

Vicky Nguyen's story does not begin with fame. It begins with flight. It begins with a choice made by two young people who risked everything for a future they could barely imagine. It begins with a boat slicing through black water under a sky thick with uncertainty.

And it begins with courage.

The fall of Saigon may have marked the end of a nation, but for Vicky's family, it marked the birth of something new. Not just a child, but a chance. Not just survival, but strength. The kind of strength that is passed from parent to child like a sacred heirloom. The kind of strength that doesn't just endure storms—it transforms them.

This is the story of a family who ran—not away from their past, but toward the promise of something better. It's the story of parents who breathed their last breath of Vietnamese air with tears in their eyes and fire in their hearts. It's the story of a girl born in the aftermath, destined not to be defined by tragedy, but to rise from it.

In the final breath of Saigon, a seed was planted. In foreign soil, watered by struggle and warmed by faith, it grew. Her name was Vicky Nguyen. And this is her story.

CHAPTER 2

PIRATES, PRAYERS, AND THE SEA THAT WOULDN'T SWALLOW US

The sea, in all its vast and indifferent beauty, has a way of testing what it means to survive. For Vicky Nguyen's family, it became both a path to freedom and a ruthless trial. After narrowly escaping the collapse of Saigon, the Nguyen family joined hundreds of other Vietnamese refugees packed onto a tiny, overburdened boat bound for uncertainty. What followed was a journey that would stretch the limits of faith, fortitude, and the fierce will to live.

Vicky's parents rarely spoke in detail about the voyage in her early years. Perhaps because to relive those moments meant revisiting trauma. Or perhaps, as is often the case with survivors, silence was the only way to contain memories too vast, too raw, too saturated in both horror and hope. But over time, the fragments emerged—often through hushed conversations, whispered prayers, or quiet tears during anniversaries no one marked on a calendar.

The boat itself was far from seaworthy. It had been built for fishing, not exodus. There were no seats, no shelter, no food storage, no sanitation. Men, women, and children sat shoulder to shoulder on wooden planks slick with seawater and desperation. Every inch was filled. Every breath was shared. The smell of fuel mingled with sweat and salt, thickening the air. Babies cried. Mothers shushed them with lullabies they barely remembered, clutching them tighter with every wave.

Day bled into night, and night into day, with no way of measuring time except by the sun's cruel arc and the ache in their bodies. The sea was not their friend. It tossed them like driftwood, swelling with storms that seemed to rise just to test them. At times, waves crashed over the edge, soaking everything and everyone. One wrong move, one slip in the wrong direction, could mean vanishing into the depths. Yet no one dared complain. The sea might not have mercy, but they could show it to each other.

Then came the pirates.

Refugee boats, slow and unprotected, were easy targets. The Nguyen family's boat was no exception. One afternoon, just as the sky began to soften into evening, a dark silhouette appeared on the horizon. Another boat. It moved fast. Too fast. There was no time to run—not that they could. Within minutes, the smaller, faster vessel pulled alongside them.

The pirates were armed. Guns glinted in the dimming light. Their faces were masked, their words foreign and sharp. They boarded without hesitation, pointing weapons and shouting commands. Vicky's mother, heavily pregnant, placed her hands over her belly instinctively. Her father stood in front of her, shielding her with the quiet bravery of a man who knew resistance would be fatal.

The pirates rifled through belongings. What little the refugees had—watches, rings, food rations, medicine—was stripped away in minutes. One woman cried when they tore a family photo from her hands. Another man was beaten when he hesitated to give up a pouch of rice. The pirates laughed, spit, and cursed, enjoying the power of cruelty.

And then, they began to scan the crowd for girls.

This was the moment every woman aboard had feared. The pirates pointed, barked orders, grabbed arms. Mothers screamed. Fathers stood, trembling with rage they couldn't act on. Vicky's parents, like many others, prayed under their breath, clutching rosaries, invoking ancestors, begging any power that could hear to intervene.

And then—suddenly, inexplicably—the pirates stopped. Something shifted. A sound, a voice, a cry from a child—no one could later agree on exactly what it was. But the pirates hesitated. One of them argued with another, gesturing angrily at the pregnant women. After a brief exchange, they threw the stolen goods into sacks, jumped back onto their boat, and sped away.

Silence fell over the boat. No one moved. No one exhaled.

Vicky's mother, heart pounding, laid a trembling hand on her belly. "God protected us," she whispered.

Some would later say it was luck. Others called it divine intervention. Whatever it was, it spared them that day. But the sea wasn't done testing them.

A few days later, a storm approached. The sky turned dark and angry, the wind howled with the fury of something ancient and hungry. Rain pelted them in sheets, soaking clothes, washing away what little warmth they'd stored. Waves towered higher than the boat, crashing down with deafening force. The boat groaned, its wooden boards straining against nature's onslaught.

People screamed. Children clung to parents. One man was swept overboard and lost within seconds. There was no time to save him, no way to even shout goodbye. Vicky's mother clutched the side of the boat with one hand and her womb with the other. Her father tied himself to the mast with a ragged rope to stay steady and help bail out water.

Through it all, they prayed. Loudly, desperately. In Vietnamese, in whispers, in sobs. Some prayed to Jesus. Others to Buddha. Some to no one in particular—just a plea into the howling void.

They prayed not to die, but more than that, to live long enough to find purpose. To give their children the chance to laugh again, to run on land that didn't reek of exile, to grow up without knowing what it meant to be hunted by sea and silence alike.

And then, as quickly as it had come, the storm passed. The sea, as if satisfied, grew calm again.

They floated for days more, living on scraps of food and hope. Many were sick. Some were unconscious. Others sang songs, softly, to keep spirits afloat. The worst had passed, but they were not yet safe.

Eventually, their boat neared the coast of Malaysia. A fishing vessel spotted them and radioed for help. Soon after, they were taken in by humanitarian workers and led to a refugee camp. The camp wasn't paradise. It was crowded, muddy, and hot. But it was land. It was stillness. It was a place to recover.

For the Nguyen family, the journey had been nearly fatal. But it was also formative. In those weeks at sea, they had lost much—dignity, possessions, and illusions. But they had also found something powerful: their unbreakable bond as a family, their capacity to endure, and the belief that no storm, no pirate, no darkness, could truly swallow them.

Later, Vicky would reflect on this chapter of her story not with bitterness, but with awe. "I was born because they survived," she once said. "And I am who I am because they never gave up."

Her parents didn't tell the story often. But when they did, their eyes always glossed over at the same part—when the pirates turned away, when the waves finally calmed, when the sun broke through the storm. These were the moments that mattered. Not because they were dramatic, but because they revealed the core of who they were: people who held on, no matter what.

And that resilience—bathed in saltwater, baptized by survival— became the foundation of everything Vicky Nguyen would later achieve. Every broadcast, every investigation, every moment of truth she chased was built on the unshakable truth that her family had once dared to believe in something bigger than fear.

They had stared into the abyss and prayed. And the sea, merciless and mighty, had chosen not to swallow them.

Their story—this chapter—is not just about danger and escape. It's about faith, in all its forms. It's about the prayers spoken into stormy skies. It's about the power of choosing to survive, over and over again, even when the world says you shouldn't have made it.

Vicky Nguyen's life began on the other side of that storm, not as a miracle, but as a continuation of courage. A legacy written not in ink, but in tide and tenacity. And this legacy, born of pirates, prayers, and a sea that couldn't break them, would become the bedrock of a life destined to inspire millions.

CHAPTER 3

THE REFUGEE CAMP DIARIES

After the tumultuous journey at sea, the Nguyen family, along with hundreds of other refugees, finally reached the shores of Malaysia. The refugee camp that became their temporary home was a sprawling labyrinth of makeshift tents and corrugated metal shelters. In this camp, life was a mix of hunger and hope, despair and determination, where every day was both a struggle and a testament to the human spirit.

The camp was a place where the boundaries between strangers blurred, and survival depended on a sense of community that was as fragile as the canvas of the tents. Here, in the midst of relentless uncertainty, Vicky Nguyen's earliest memories began to take shape. Even as a baby, she was surrounded by the soft murmurs of families who had lost everything, yet clung to every ounce of hope they could muster.

In the beginning, the days were long and overwhelming. The refugees arrived exhausted, their bodies weak from the relentless waves and their hearts heavy with loss. Hunger gnawed at everyone, and food was scarce. A thin soup of rice and a few vegetables were all that was available to stave off starvation. Yet, despite these hardships, there was an unspoken understanding among the camp's inhabitants: they had to keep going. Every meal, however meager, was a small victory.

Vicky's parents, like many others, set aside moments in their day for quiet prayers. They gathered in small groups near the communal water tap, voices low and measured, as if speaking too loudly might summon the ghosts of their past. These moments of prayer were not just appeals for divine intervention; they were also expressions of gratitude. Even in the depths of hunger and fatigue, there was an undercurrent of thanks for another day survived.

Amid the desperation, laughter became an unexpected medicine. In one corner of the camp, under the shade of a rickety tarpaulin, a group of older refugees would share stories of their youth, often with a wry humor that defied the bleak surroundings. They recalled small, absurd moments from life in Vietnam—jokes about the peculiar taste of street food, comical misunderstandings in the marketplace, and even the idiosyncrasies of local customs. Their laughter was contagious, a reminder that even in exile, the spark of life could not be fully extinguished.

Vicky's father, a man of few words but deep conviction, would sometimes smile quietly as he listened to these anecdotes. He rarely recounted his own experiences; instead, he found solace in the laughter of others. It was a silent acknowledgment that while the camp was a place of suffering, it was also a crucible where resilience was forged through shared humanity.

Within the camp, community was more than just a survival mechanism—it was a lifeline. Neighbors looked after each other, sharing not only food but also their stories and dreams. Every evening, as the sun dipped below the horizon and cast long shadows over the dusty paths, groups of refugees would gather around small fires. There, they would exchange tales of past glories, hardships endured, and the unyielding hope for a better tomorrow.

One evening, as a cool breeze offered a brief respite from the oppressive heat, an elderly man named Mr. Dinh stood up in the center of a circle of listeners. His voice, though frail, carried the weight of decades. "We have lost so much," he said, his eyes misty with memories, "but remember, even when all seems lost, our spirit remains unbroken. We laugh not because our hearts are light, but because we must; it is our defiance against despair."

His words resonated deeply with everyone present. Even young children, who had grown up amidst the harsh realities of displacement, would pause to listen, their innocent eyes reflecting a glimmer of understanding. It was in these moments that the camp transformed from a place of mere survival into a community where shared suffering was met with shared strength.

The daily routine in the camp was marked by both monotony and unpredictability. Mornings began early with the call of a makeshift bell—often just a metal pipe struck against a tin can—that signaled the start of another day. People lined up to collect water, a precious commodity in a place where every drop was rationed carefully. Then, it was time to queue for food, where a bowl of rice and a small serving of vegetables was distributed with as much order as the chaotic circumstances allowed.

For many, the waiting was excruciating. Vicky's mother, with her gentle eyes and quiet determination, would sometimes stand in line for hours, her thoughts drifting to a time before war, before the need to flee. In her mind, she recalled the vibrant markets of Saigon, the tantalizing aroma of fresh herbs, and the sounds of life that once filled their home. Those memories, though bittersweet, served as a reminder of what they had lost and what they still hoped to reclaim.

Despite the pervasive hardship, there were also moments of unexpected kindness. Volunteers from international organizations arrived periodically, bringing with them not just food and medicine, but also small tokens of normalcy—a few toys for the children, a packet of seeds to plant in a communal garden, or a radio that played distant news and music from home. These gifts, though modest, carried the promise of a world beyond the camp, where life could one day return to some semblance of order.

In the evenings, as the communal fires flickered against the encroaching darkness, children's laughter would sometimes pierce the silence. They played games that mimicked the world outside the camp—a world they had only heard about in whispered stories and old photographs. They chased each other around makeshift tents, their feet kicking up dust and their voices full of hope. For a few precious hours, the burdens of hunger and exile were forgotten, replaced by the pure joy of play.

In one such moment, as the firelight danced across the faces of the gathered, a young girl named Linh approached a group of older children with a makeshift toy—a wooden top carved from a discarded piece of wood. "Watch this," she said, her voice trembling with excitement. With a deft flick of her wrist, the top spun rapidly, its movement mesmerizing in the firelight. The children clapped and cheered, and for that brief moment, the hardships of the day were transformed into a celebration of life's small wonders.

Vicky, even as an infant cradled in her mother's arms, absorbed these impressions. Although she could not yet understand the full gravity of their situation, the camp's rhythms—its hardships, its communal bonds, and its bursts of laughter—became the first chapters of her own life's narrative. In the soft murmur of shared stories and the whispered promises of a better future, she found the seeds of resilience that would later define her career as a journalist and advocate.

Over time, as the refugees slowly began to stabilize within the camp, routines evolved. Makeshift schools were established where children learned basic lessons in Vietnamese and rudimentary English. For the adults, the camp became a place of quiet reflection and pragmatic adaptation. They exchanged news from their homeland, debated the best ways to preserve what little they had, and dreamed collectively of repatriation or resettlement. In these shared spaces, the camp was not just a temporary holding place—it was a crucible of cultural continuity and transformation.

The refugee camp diaries of that period, though not formally written at the time, were etched into the minds of those who lived through it. Each day was recorded in gestures, in whispered conversations during the night, and in the silent understanding between neighbors. These were the days when survival was measured not in hours or minutes, but in the strength of community bonds and the resilience of the human spirit. It was in this crucible of suffering and solidarity that the identity of the Vietnamese diaspora was forged—a testament to the enduring hope that even in the face of overwhelming adversity, laughter and love could flourish.

For Vicky Nguyen, these early experiences in the refugee camp would later inform her work as a journalist. The blend of pain and humor she witnessed, the quiet determination that saw people through the darkest nights, and the unyielding bond of community—all these elements became part of her narrative voice. They taught her that every story, no matter how tragic, held within it the potential for redemption and renewal.

Looking back on those days, one could almost hear the camp itself speaking—a soft murmur carried on the wind, filled with the echoes of countless voices. It spoke of hunger and loss, yes, but also of courage and the undying belief that tomorrow would bring a new beginning. It was a place where survival was not just an act of physical endurance, but a profound expression of faith in the human capacity to overcome.

In the quiet moments of dusk, when the camp settled into a fragile calm and the only sound was the distant hum of generators, one could sense a collective heartbeat—a rhythm of life that pulsed beneath the surface of despair. It was in that heartbeat that Vicky Nguyen found her first lesson in storytelling: that every life, no matter how fraught with struggle, is a story worth telling.

Thus, the refugee camp diaries are not merely records of a difficult chapter in history. They are living testaments to the resilience of the human spirit. They remind us that even in the most inhospitable conditions, there exists a spark of hope—a spark that can ignite laughter, foster community, and ultimately, inspire the will to rise again.

For the Nguyen family, and for countless others who endured similar hardships, the camp was a crucible where sorrow was tempered by solidarity and despair was met with determination. It was here that Vicky Nguyen's journey took its first true steps, as the echoes of shared hardship and unexpected joy carved an indelible mark on her soul. And it is from this legacy—of hunger and community, of survival and laughter—that her lifelong mission to give voice to the voiceless was born.

CHAPTER 4

FROM TENT TO TEXAS

The boat had barely come to a stop before the chaos of the refugee camp swallowed up Vicky and her family, their first steps on American soil. For Vicky, these early moments in a foreign land would forever be tied to the smell of freshly cut grass, the overwhelming brightness of Texas sunshine, and the sharp bite of uncertainty. It was a new chapter in their story—one of survival, reinvention, and the unspoken promise of hope.

But it wasn't a neat transition. There was no clear-cut moment of arrival—no warm embrace from a welcoming community. The journey from the cramped, overcrowded boat to the sterile, sprawling refugee camps was an arduous one. And though they had left the violence and unrest of Vietnam behind, they quickly found that the challenges of being an immigrant were far from over.

The first few months were disorienting. The sprawling refugee camp was a world unlike anything the family had known. The tents, stretched taut against the arid Texas landscape, created a temporary home for hundreds of families. Vicky, only a toddler at the time, would have little memory of the logistics of survival. What would stay with her were the sounds and smells—the distinct clinking of metal pots, the hushed murmurs of people speaking in Vietnamese, and the overwhelming taste of fear and uncertainty that filled the air like dust.

For her parents, the promise of the American dream felt as distant as the moon. Their lives had been uprooted so violently, their futures torn apart so thoroughly, that simply standing on the edge of a new world seemed impossible. Yet there they were, in a place that would eventually become home, but initially, it was nothing more than an alien expanse of tents, barbed wire, and sun-baked earth.

Vicky's parents, both hardened by war and loss, were also determined. Her father, despite the invisible scars left by his own war experience, was nothing if not resilient. He saw his children's future in a way they could not—an image of possibility framed by the red, white, and blue that waved above them in the heat of Texas.

Assimilation wasn't something they could fully comprehend. They had been through too much to simply "fit in." The language barrier was the first wall they faced. It was a harsh wall that seemed to separate their old world from the new one in ways that were hard to articulate, let alone overcome. Her father's English was rudimentary, and Vicky's mother barely spoke a word of it. Every interaction was a small battle. When they went to buy food or find clothes, it was as if the language itself stood between them and their survival.

Vicky herself, though far too young to understand these intricacies, would come to realize that language was both a bridge and a barrier. Her earliest memories, hazy and fragmented as they were, involved watching her parents stumble through these interactions, navigating a world in which they were strangers, their accents thick, their syntax unfamiliar.

The refugee camp was a temporary pit stop, but it was long enough to plant the seeds of cultural dissonance. Vicky's world had become divided into two: the world of her family, rooted in the familiar sounds of Vietnamese, the smells of rice and fish sauce, the rituals of family, and the world outside—unrecognizable, a language she couldn't understand, a culture that felt as foreign as the land itself.

Her parents did everything they could to protect her from the harsher realities of this world. They would speak to her in Vietnamese as often as they could, telling stories of home—of their life in Vietnam before the war, of the small village they had left behind, of the family and friends they may never see again. They told her of the life they dreamed of having here—of safety, of opportunity, of a future in which they could rebuild and thrive.

But Vicky wasn't immune to the culture shock. The sounds, the sights, the strange people who didn't look like her, spoke like her, or eat like her—it was all part of a world that she had no choice but to learn. Her first memory of America wasn't one of happiness or warmth—it was confusion. The world around her seemed so big, and she was so small.

The playground at the camp was one of the first places where Vicky would begin to form connections to the new world. She was drawn to other children, despite the language barrier, but communication was awkward, stilted. Children would speak to her in a language she didn't yet understand, pointing at toys, making gestures that were unfamiliar. It was there, in the clumsy exchanges with kids who spoke a different language, that Vicky began her early lessons in what it meant to be both Vietnamese and American.

The moment of transformation, when she began to speak English, didn't come all at once. It happened in small, barely noticeable ways—when a kind American woman at the refugee camp taught her the English words for things, or when she overheard her father trying to read a book in English, struggling but determined. The language was a strange thing, a puzzle to be pieced together, but slowly, it clicked.

Vicky would never forget the feeling of saying her first English word—"cat." She would repeat it over and over again, fascinated by how her mouth formed the strange sounds. It was a bridge into a world that had previously felt so out of reach, and with that word, Vicky took one more step toward assimilation, one more step toward becoming a part of the American fabric.

It wasn't easy, though. The fight for assimilation was a constant one. The family would move from the camp into a small apartment in Texas, a place that would become their home for the next few years. For Vicky's parents, it was a time of quiet struggle. They worked multiple jobs, often at the expense of sleep, health, and time together. But they did it because they believed—no, they *knew*—that this was their chance. This was their shot at a new life, and they would stop at nothing to make it work.

Vicky grew up in the dichotomy of two worlds. At home, she was Vietnamese. Her parents ensured that their culture was kept alive, from the food they ate to the values they instilled in her. But when she stepped outside, she was a little girl in Texas, grappling with her identity, trying to understand what it meant to be both.

Her earliest memories as a Vietnamese-American child were marked by this tension—by the constant back-and-forth between her heritage and the expectations of her new home. It wasn't always easy to reconcile the two. Sometimes, her classmates would make fun of her lunch, calling it strange or exotic. At other times, they'd comment on her accent, or ask if she had "fresh-off-the-boat" roots. These moments were painful, but they also pushed Vicky to define who she was on her own terms.

Looking back on those early years, Vicky recognizes how profoundly those moments shaped her sense of identity. The fusion of two cultures, the constant negotiation of what it meant to be Vietnamese and American, was a theme that would play out throughout her life. It would inform her career as a journalist, where she would use her voice to tell stories that bridged divides, that illuminated the struggles and triumphs of immigrants, and that celebrated the resilience of those who dared to rise.

From tent to Texas, the journey was never simple, but it was rich with the kind of growth and transformation that defines the immigrant experience. Vicky's story was just beginning, and though the road ahead was long and uncertain, she would never forget the lessons she learned in those early days. The pain of assimilation, the sacrifice of her parents, and the struggle to find her place in a new world would all be integral to her rise as a journalist—and as a woman who, despite the odds, became an anchor in a world she had once only dreamed of understanding.

CHAPTER 5

PHO, FULL HOUSE, AND FITTING IN

Vicky Nguyen's first lessons in English didn't come from a textbook or a classroom—at least not in the traditional sense. They came from a place far more entertaining and, at times, much more confusing: the television. It was here, sitting on the threadbare carpet of her family's living room in their small Texas apartment, that she would become an unlikely student of the American sitcom. She didn't understand most of the words at first, but somehow, the sitcoms had a way of speaking to her.

Pho, Full House, and the endless cycle of 90s TV shows would become her unwitting teachers. It all started innocently enough. Her parents, desperate to learn English, would watch shows like *Full House*, *The Fresh Prince of Bel-Air*, and *Family Ties*—anything that might help them communicate better in their new world. At the time, Vicky had no idea that these goofy characters, with their silly catchphrases and exaggerated emotions, would soon become her linguistic lifeline.

She would sit beside her parents, absorbing English as best she could. But the struggle was real. "How come they keep saying 'You got it, dude'?" she'd ask, puzzled. Her parents, equally confused, shrugged and smiled. The line had stuck, but the meaning was still elusive. "I don't know, Vicky, maybe it's something funny in the show?" They weren't wrong. The jokes may have been lost in translation, but the warmth, the laughter, and the familiar rhythm of family life felt universal. In time, Vicky would start piecing it together—slowly at first, then with more confidence.

The sitcoms taught her more than just vocabulary; they provided a window into an unfamiliar world. The Duncans of *Full House* and the Banks family of *The Fresh Prince* weren't just amusing—they were examples of a family life Vicky could only dream of. The affection they shared, the inside jokes, the easy camaraderie—they spoke to the part of Vicky that longed for connection, for belonging in this strange new world.

But the humor was both a bridge and a barrier. Vicky could mimic the phrases, but she was far from fluent. Her accent still clung stubbornly to her words, turning "You got it, dude!" into something that sounded more like "You got eed, doo?" She would hear laughter from the TV screen and wonder if anyone would ever laugh at her jokes. She would laugh at their jokes, but only because the characters' faces would scrunch up in a way that made it clear it was time to laugh.

Even as she tried to figure out the nuances of American humor, school was where the real challenges of her identity began to take shape.

School was a battleground of sorts—a place where, every day, Vicky would try to negotiate between the world of her parents and the world outside. It was where she was supposed to fit in but often felt like she couldn't. Her classmates didn't look like her. They didn't speak like her. And they certainly didn't eat like her.

Lunchtime was one of the most awkward parts of the day. Vicky's mother, ever the perfectionist, would pack her with a plastic container full of pho—a steaming bowl of noodles, broth, and meat that smelled distinctly different from the peanut butter sandwiches of her classmates. Vicky knew it was different. She could see the way her friends would wrinkle their noses when the scent hit the air. Some would ask, "What's that smell?" while others would giggle, calling it "weird."

In these moments, Vicky would shrink inside herself. Her lunch—her mother's food, her comfort—felt like a target for ridicule. She'd sit quietly, trying not to draw attention, while her friends opened their neatly packaged sandwiches. The food was a symbol of everything that set her apart, and the sting of being different hit hard in those moments. It wasn't until later that Vicky realized those differences weren't something to hide but something to celebrate. But in elementary school, that lesson was still far from clear.

Her accent was another obstacle. While her English was improving, it was still far from perfect. There were words that didn't roll off her tongue the way they should. She still mixed up sounds, blending English and Vietnamese into a jumbled hybrid that her classmates didn't understand. "What?" they'd ask when she tried to explain something, their faces scrunched in confusion. It was frustrating, but it also became an unintentional lesson in patience—for both her and her classmates. In a world that prized clarity and ease, Vicky was learning to navigate the messy space in between languages, between cultures.

And yet, despite the awkwardness, there were small triumphs. One day, her teacher asked the class to write an essay about their favorite food. Vicky's classmates were quick to hand in their papers about pizza, hamburgers, and macaroni and cheese. Vicky, without missing a beat, wrote about pho. It was a declaration of her identity, even if it was just one word on a page.

Her teacher was curious. "Vicky," she asked after reading the essay, "what is pho?" Vicky smiled, grateful for the opportunity to explain. "It's a noodle soup," she said, "but it's different from what you might think. The broth takes a long time to make, and it's really flavorful. My mom makes it really well." The teacher smiled back. The other kids leaned in, intrigued by the foreign food. It was a moment of connection, a bridge between cultures.

These small wins—these moments where Vicky took pride in what made her different—were the ones that gradually helped her find her place. They didn't erase the challenges, but they gave her a sense of pride that couldn't be taken away. As the years passed, Vicky would learn how to stand in the space between her Vietnamese heritage and her American life, embracing both with humor, humility, and resilience.

Her identity as a Vietnamese-American child was one of constant negotiation. She was torn between two worlds, trying to make sense of the disparate expectations. At school, she was the girl with the accent, the girl with the strange lunches. But at home, she was Vicky, the daughter of hardworking immigrants who had fled a war-torn country for a better life. Her mother's strict rules about education clashed with her desire to fit in with her peers. Her father's quiet sacrifices weren't always understood by her friends, who couldn't fathom what it meant to leave everything behind in search of something better.

But through it all, Vicky remained resilient. She discovered that humor was one of the most powerful tools in her arsenal. By laughing at herself, by seeing the absurdity in her experiences, she could turn what might have been embarrassing moments into stories of triumph. And in those moments, she learned that fitting in didn't mean erasing her identity—it meant embracing it fully.

As Vicky grew older, she would look back at those awkward moments with fondness. They were the building blocks of who she would become—the confident, sharp-witted journalist who would later tell stories of resilience, identity, and transformation. The awkwardness of childhood was the soil in which her humor, her intelligence, and her compassion would take root.

Pho, Full House, and fitting in were more than just part of Vicky's journey—they were metaphors for the complex dance of assimilation, identity, and belonging. Through them, she learned that the real triumph wasn't about fitting in—it was about standing tall in the space between two worlds, laughing at the journey, and finding the beauty in both.

CHAPTER 6

GROWING UP WITH GRIT – EDUCATION, EXPECTATIONS & EXTRA RICE

Vicky Nguyen's childhood was a study in contrasts: a family uprooted by war and replanting itself in the fertile soil of the American Dream, struggling not just for survival, but for a place at the table. Her parents, immigrants who had come from Vietnam in search of better opportunities, held one universal belief that would drive their daughter's upbringing—education was the key. But to them, it wasn't just about good grades. It was about survival, reinvention, and the weight of their own sacrifices. Vicky's future was not just her own; it was the hope of their entire family. The pressure to succeed was immense, and it would shape her into the woman she would eventually become.

Her parents' expectations were not subtle. They were clear, unwavering, and demanding. "You want to make something of yourself," her father would often say, "You need to work hard, study hard." And hard work, to them, wasn't just about putting in time; it was about pushing beyond limits, overcoming obstacles, and embracing the future that had, for so long, seemed impossible. Education, in their eyes, was the most direct route to a new life, a better life, and ultimately, the American Dream.

Vicky remembers coming home from school with a report card that she knew would bring both pride and worry to her parents. It wasn't that her grades weren't good—Vicky was a diligent student, driven by both internal ambition and the weight of her parents' expectations. But there was always a sense that it could be better, that there was more to be done, more to prove. Her parents saw her academic performance as a reflection of their own success in America. If she did well, they had done well. If she faltered, so did they.

"Why only an A minus? You could do better," her mother would say, shaking her head as Vicky placed her report card on the kitchen table. There was no applause for grades that were simply "good enough." Perfection was expected, and as a child, that pressure often felt overwhelming. But Vicky learned early on that this wasn't a reflection of a lack of love. It was an expression of hope, of their desire to see her rise higher than they ever could. Every little victory was hard-earned for her parents, who had given up so much to come to America. Her successes, in their eyes, were part of their redemption.

The sacrifices were never far from Vicky's mind. Her parents worked long hours in low-wage jobs—her father in construction, her mother in a factory. They were physically and emotionally drained by the time they came home, but still, they found ways to drill into their daughter the importance of academic excellence. It was a ritual, almost religious in its consistency. Every evening, as the sun dipped below the horizon, Vicky would sit at the kitchen table, the hum of the fluorescent light above and the smell of rice and pork filling the air, and study—always study.

And then there was the rice. Rice was always there—at every meal, in every corner of their home, a symbol of sustenance, survival, and culture. Her mother would cook extra rice, knowing that they would always need more. The rice was a reminder of where they came from and what they had left behind, but also of what they had worked for, what they had built from scratch. It wasn't just food; it was a part of their story, part of their resilience.

But Vicky's academic life was not just shaped by expectations—it was also shaped by struggles. She fought for every inch of academic success, at times feeling like an outsider in a world that didn't quite understand her. She had learned to speak English, yes, but it had never quite felt like it was her own language. There were moments in class when Vicky would falter, when she couldn't understand the instructions, or when she felt lost in the sea of textbooks and assignments. She didn't have the luxury of slipping under the radar; her parents' eyes were on her constantly, reminding her that failure wasn't an option.

It was a struggle that would only get more complicated as Vicky grew older. In high school, when she became more aware of her identity as a Vietnamese-American, she began to grapple with the conflicting expectations of her culture and the reality of being a teenager in America. She found herself caught between two worlds: the one her parents had worked so hard to create for her, and the one she was trying to navigate as an American girl.

Vicky's classmates were far more interested in parties, hanging out, and high school drama than in homework and grades. While they were out having fun, she was at home, cramming for the next test, trying to meet her parents' unspoken demands for perfection. She would spend hours pouring over textbooks, only to be met with the same question from her mother: "Did you study enough?" The internal pressure was just as heavy as the external.

But in these moments, Vicky found her resilience. She started learning how to balance the two worlds. She began to internalize that while her parents' expectations were undeniably high, they were also the driving force behind her success. They weren't simply asking for better grades—they were asking for a better life. Her academic struggles and triumphs were their triumphs too. In every test score, in every essay written, in every grade that moved up a notch, Vicky was giving back to them. She was doing this for herself, for her family, and for the dream they had all built together.

It was during these high school years that Vicky began to show signs of the journalistic curiosity that would one day propel her into her career. She wasn't aware of it at the time, but her insatiable need for information, her tendency to ask questions, and her deep desire to understand the world around her were all signs that she was developing the very skills that would shape her future. It wasn't enough just to learn the facts; she wanted to understand why things were the way they were, to uncover the story behind the story.

One of her earliest journalistic experiences happened almost by accident. Vicky's high school had a small student newspaper, and one day, she decided to write a piece about the struggles of immigrant students. She wasn't interested in the usual fluff pieces about homecoming dances or prom dress shopping—Vicky wanted to tell a story that mattered. She interviewed her classmates, many of whom shared similar stories of navigating life between two cultures, and she wrote an article that reflected the complexity of their experiences. It was raw, emotional, and thought-provoking, and it caught the attention of her teacher.

"Vicky, this is really good," her teacher told her. "You've got a knack for this. Have you considered writing for a larger audience?"

At the time, Vicky wasn't sure what she wanted to do with her life, but in that moment, she felt the spark. Writing wasn't just about grades. It wasn't about meeting expectations. It was about telling the truth, about digging deeper into the human experience, about sharing stories that needed to be heard.

In hindsight, Vicky would later realize that it wasn't just academic success that had driven her to that point. It was the grit she had learned from her parents, the resilience they had instilled in her. Her mother's constant reminder that "extra rice" was a symbol of their determination was a metaphor for the extra effort she would put into everything she did—whether it was studying, writing, or pursuing a career in journalism. Her parents' belief that there was always room for more—more effort, more learning, more work—became the foundation for her own success.

Vicky's journey was never just about academic achievement. It was about something deeper—a drive to be more, to break through barriers, and to prove that no matter where you start, you can rise. The pressures of growing up with immigrant parents, the expectations that sometimes felt too heavy to bear, would all ultimately shape her into the determined, insightful journalist she would become. Her struggles and successes in school were not just the result of hard work—they were the foundation for a career built on telling the stories of others, on uncovering truths, and on finding the strength to rise above it all.

CHAPTER 7

THE RISE OF A VOICE

Vicky Nguyen didn't set out to be a journalist because she thought it would be glamorous. She didn't enter the field because of a burning desire to be on TV or to make headlines. What drew her to journalism was something far deeper, something rooted in her upbringing as a child of Vietnamese refugees who came to the United States seeking a new life. Her journey into the world of news reporting wasn't just about finding a career; it was about finding her voice—and using it to give a voice to others who, like her family, had once been silenced or overlooked.

Breaking into journalism was not an easy feat, and for Vicky, it was an uphill battle. The newsroom was a battleground—fierce, competitive, and not always welcoming. The odds were stacked against her from the start. As an Asian-American woman, she faced challenges that her peers didn't. There was the weight of representation, the cultural isolation, and the unspoken pressure to prove herself in an industry where diversity was still, even in the late 2000s, a work in progress. But Vicky was used to fighting for her place. She had been doing that all her life, ever since her family had arrived in the United States as refugees, navigating the complexities of their new life while holding on to their past.

Her first job in journalism came after years of sweat, persistence, and the inevitable string of internships. She had attended college with a focus on communication, driven by the belief that journalism could be a vehicle for change. It wasn't just about the stories themselves; it was about telling them with integrity, telling them with heart, and telling them with a commitment to truth. That was something Vicky learned from her parents, who had risked everything to start anew in a foreign land. They'd instilled in her a deep respect for honesty, hard work, and the importance of telling one's story.

Her first major break came when she landed a position as a reporter at a local news station. It wasn't a glamorous job, and it wasn't exactly a high-profile position, but it was a foot in the door—a place to prove herself. Her first stories were small, but Vicky poured everything into them. She had a knack for getting the details right, for capturing the human side of a story. She understood, perhaps better than most, that the real story wasn't always in the facts and figures; it was in the people behind them. This ability to see the humanity in every story made her stand out.

But it wasn't all smooth sailing. Her first year in the newsroom was filled with challenges that stretched her patience, her resilience, and her sense of self. There were the long hours, the impossible deadlines, and the pressure to produce high-quality work in an industry that thrived on the fast-paced news cycle. There were the moments of self-doubt, the voices in her head asking if she was good enough, if she was really cut out for this. There were the newsroom politics—the unspoken rules, the behind-the-scenes drama, and the constant competition. But Vicky, fueled by a mix of ambition and determination, pushed forward. She made her mark with stories that mattered, stories that revealed something important about the world and the people in it.

Behind the scenes of her first major stories, Vicky learned how to navigate the complexities of reporting. She discovered that being a good journalist wasn't just about being able to write a good lead or nail an interview. It was about being persistent, about knocking on doors, about digging deeper, and about earning the trust of the people whose stories she was telling. She learned the importance of listening, of paying attention to the nuances that others might overlook. She understood that a reporter's job wasn't just to gather information—it was to connect the dots, to make sense of the chaos, and to give context to a world that often felt out of control.

One of her first major stories was an in-depth investigation into a local housing crisis, an issue that hit close to home for Vicky. She had grown up in a working-class neighborhood where many families struggled to make ends meet. She had seen firsthand the impact of inadequate housing, and she knew that this story was important—not just for her career, but for the people who would benefit from the exposure. It was a story that required countless interviews, hours of research, and the courage to stand up to powerful interests. But Vicky's drive to make a difference pushed her through. When the story aired, it received widespread attention, and Vicky was hailed for her thoroughness and her ability to present complex issues in a way that made them accessible to the average viewer.

For Vicky, the story wasn't just about shining a light on a problem. It was about humanizing the issue, about showing the faces of the people affected by the housing crisis. She wanted the audience to see the people behind the statistics—to understand their struggles, their dreams, and their resilience. This story was a turning point in her career. It showed her that journalism was not just a job for her; it was a calling. She realized that she had a responsibility to use her platform to amplify voices that were often ignored or overlooked.

But with success came new challenges. As Vicky's career progressed, she started to realize that the world of journalism, particularly the broadcast media world, was still dominated by a very narrow and homogenous group of people. As an Asian-American woman, she often found herself in spaces where she was one of the few people of color. She encountered subtle and not-so-subtle forms of bias, both from her colleagues and from the public. There were the jokes that weren't really jokes, the comments about her accent (despite speaking flawless English), and the constant need to prove herself in ways her white colleagues didn't.

One of the toughest lessons Vicky learned was that in the media industry, especially in the early years of her career, being an Asian-American woman often meant being typecast. There were certain stories she was expected to cover—stories related to Asian communities, immigrant issues, or the occasional "human interest" piece about a heartwarming family reunion or a small business owner. The subtle implication was that her identity as a Vietnamese-American somehow defined the kinds of stories she was "qualified" to tell.

But Vicky never let these limitations define her. Instead, she used them as fuel. She understood that she could write and report on any topic, that her experiences as a Vietnamese-American woman didn't limit her; they enhanced her perspective. She pushed back against the stereotypes, carving out a space for herself in an industry that, at times, seemed unwilling to make room for someone like her. Over time, Vicky became known for her insightful, compassionate, and fearless reporting. She was no longer just the "Asian reporter"—she was a journalist who could cover anything, from politics to human rights to breaking news, with a level of professionalism and skill that earned her the respect of her peers.

Her rise in the media world was slow, but steady. She became known for her sharp instincts, her meticulous research, and her ability to connect with people. And as she rose through the ranks, she never lost sight of her original mission—to use journalism to make a difference, to shine a light on stories that mattered, and to give a voice to those who had been silenced.

Vicky's journey as a journalist was more than just a career—it was a calling. It was about breaking through barriers, pushing back against the stereotypes, and using her voice to tell stories that needed to be heard. And as she continued to rise, she carried with her the lessons she had learned from her parents: the importance of hard work, the value of education, and the unshakable belief that one voice, no matter how small, can make a difference in the world.

CHAPTER 8

NBC, NATIONAL SPOTLIGHT & NEVER FORGETTING HOME

Vicky Nguyen's journey from a refugee child to becoming a national correspondent for NBC was not the culmination of a simple dream—it was the embodiment of grit, ambition, and an unshakable sense of purpose. In a profession where success often feels like a distant, improbable goal, Vicky managed to carve out her own path, balancing her career with a deep commitment to the issues that shaped her identity. From the day she first set foot in a newsroom to becoming an established face on national television, Vicky never lost sight of the lessons her parents taught her: resilience, integrity, and the importance of telling stories that matter.

Her career trajectory wasn't one marked by a series of grandiose steps. It was built on moments of quiet determination, late nights spent chasing stories, and unrelenting commitment to her craft. By the time Vicky was tapped to become an NBC correspondent, she had already proven herself as a journalist with a distinct voice— one that was not just concerned with breaking news, but with uncovering the human side of every story, especially the stories that often went untold. She had built a reputation for herself, not just as a reporter but as a truth-teller, someone unafraid to ask the tough questions and to challenge the narratives that dominated the airwaves.

Becoming an NBC correspondent was a dream come true, but it didn't come without its own set of challenges. The transition from local newsrooms to a national platform was jarring, and Vicky had to navigate the expectations of a much larger audience. The stakes were higher now—every story, every broadcast, every segment had the potential to shape national discourse. But as much as the job became more demanding, Vicky embraced the challenge. She wasn't just representing herself now; she was representing her community, her family, and the millions of other immigrants whose stories had yet to be fully told.

One of the first things that struck her when she made the leap to national reporting was the weight of visibility. In a profession that already demanded a strong sense of self, Vicky now had to contend with being in the national spotlight—something she'd never anticipated. She was no longer just Vicky the local reporter from a small station; she was Vicky Nguyen, the Vietnamese-American journalist with a national platform. There was an added pressure to succeed, to be a role model for others in her community, and to prove that someone with her background—someone who was not white, not from an elite pedigree, and not from a traditional media family—could rise to the top.

But instead of retreating from this responsibility, Vicky leaned into it. She knew that her presence in the media could open doors for others, that her story could give hope to young people of color who had always dreamed of seeing someone who looked like them in the national news. She also knew that with her growing platform came an opportunity—an opportunity to tackle issues that mattered, issues that had been too often ignored or misrepresented.

Throughout her time at NBC, Vicky made it a point to highlight stories that addressed pressing social issues, including the rise of racism, misinformation, and the complex dynamics of American identity. Her commitment to these topics wasn't just professional—

it was deeply personal. Having grown up as an immigrant, she had witnessed firsthand the power of misinformation, the damaging effects of racism, and the struggles of being marginalized. She knew that in order to build a more just society, the stories of those who had been left behind—stories like hers—needed to be told.

One of the most powerful examples of Vicky's work in this area came when she covered the rise of anti-Asian hate crimes during the COVID-19 pandemic. As the virus spread, so did the scapegoating and vilification of Asian communities. Vicky felt a deep responsibility to report on the spike in violence against Asian Americans, especially because, for the first time in her life, she was hearing people spew hate about her people on a national scale. It was a moment that felt personal, and she used her platform to highlight the struggles of those affected by these attacks, shedding light on the complexities of racism that went beyond surface-level conversations.

Vicky's reporting was incisive, compassionate, and unflinching in its portrayal of the harsh realities faced by many Asian Americans. But what made her work stand out was her ability to humanize these stories. Instead of focusing solely on statistics or newsworthy incidents, Vicky brought her audience into the lives of the people who were being impacted. She told the stories of the elderly immigrants who were attacked while walking to their local grocery store, the young people who felt a sense of fear and alienation for the first time in their lives, and the families who had been left reeling by violence that struck too close to home.

Through her reporting, Vicky did something that was far more than just delivering the news: she helped people understand the emotional and psychological toll of living in a society where hate was becoming more normalized. She used her platform to combat misinformation, presenting facts and truth in the face of baseless accusations and stereotypes. She spoke out against the dangerous rhetoric that was infecting public discourse, using her position not just as a journalist, but as an advocate for truth and justice.

Despite the national spotlight, Vicky never forgot where she came from. Her heritage remained at the heart of everything she did, both personally and professionally. She always made it a point to honor the sacrifices her parents made to give her the opportunities she had. The core values of her upbringing—family, resilience, and a commitment to doing good—continued to guide her work, even as she became more well-known.

Her parents' influence was ever-present, even as her career took off. When she'd return home to visit them, she would often sit around the dinner table with her mother and father, reminiscing about their early days in America. They would talk about their struggles, about the language barriers, and the constant feeling of being outsiders. But they would also talk about their dreams for her, how proud they were to see her doing well, how they never lost hope that their sacrifices had been worth it.

In these quiet moments of reflection, Vicky found herself reconnecting with the reasons she became a journalist in the first place: to tell the stories that matter, to amplify voices that had been marginalized, and to never forget the importance of staying grounded in her roots.

Vicky knew that she had made it to a place in her career that few people like her ever reached. But she also knew that the journey wasn't over. As she looked toward the future, she realized that her work wasn't just about the stories she had already told—it was about the stories she still had yet to uncover. There were still so many voices left unheard, so many truths left untold. And as long as she had a platform, she would continue to shine a light on them.

Her journey was a testament to the power of perseverance, the importance of staying true to one's values, and the necessity of using one's voice for good. For Vicky Nguyen, being a journalist was never just about reporting the news—it was about giving a voice to those who needed it most. It was about staying rooted in her heritage while navigating the ever-changing tides of a career that demanded both resilience and vulnerability. In the national spotlight, Vicky never forgot home.

CHAPTER 9

HUMOR IN HARDSHIP

Laughter, Vicky Nguyen would tell you, is a weapon, a shield, and a life raft all rolled into one. As a child who came to America as a "boat baby," she quickly learned the art of using humor to navigate through a world that felt foreign, overwhelming, and often hostile. It wasn't just about cracking jokes or making people laugh—it was about finding lightness in the darkest of situations and using that light to keep going.

When she first arrived in the United States, Vicky faced a barrage of challenges that could have easily crushed her spirit. As a young girl who spoke no English, the culture shock was overwhelming. The language barrier left her feeling isolated, alien, and disconnected from her peers. But her sharp wit and infectious sense of humor became her armor. It was the one thing she could control in a world where so much felt beyond her grasp.

Vicky often reflects on how humor was her first language in America, even before she could string a sentence together in English. "You don't need words to make someone laugh," she says. "It's a universal language that can bridge any gap." Her early memories are filled with moments where she would mimic the accents of her classmates, trying to fit in while also deflecting the sting of being different. She would make jokes about the way her family ate, or how they struggled with English. It was her way of confronting the awkwardness head-on, of acknowledging her differences without letting them define her.

In many ways, humor became a survival tactic—especially as the family struggled with the trauma of their refugee journey. Vicky's parents, who had lost everything in Vietnam, were determined to build a better life for their children, but the process was anything but easy. They faced hardship at every turn—economic challenges, racism, and the constant reminder that they were strangers in a new land. Yet, despite the weight of their struggles, Vicky's parents maintained an incredible sense of humor. They made light of their hardships, often joking about their broken English or their missteps in American culture.

One of Vicky's favorite memories is of her father, who, despite his own lack of formal education, always found a way to make the family laugh. He would tell stories about how he'd butchered the English language at work, often mispronouncing words to the point of absurdity. Vicky recalls how her father would laugh at himself, turning the awkwardness of the situation into something comical rather than shameful. "It's better to laugh than cry," he would say, and those words stayed with her.

For Vicky, humor became the bridge between two worlds—her old world in Vietnam and her new one in America. It allowed her to acknowledge the hardship she faced without succumbing to it. It became a tool for processing trauma, a way to make sense of the seemingly senseless. By laughing at the absurdities of life, Vicky learned to hold the pain and the joy together, without letting either one overwhelm her.

As an adult, Vicky continued to use humor as a way to cope with the challenges she faced in her professional life. As a journalist, she often encountered stories that were difficult to process—stories about racism, inequality, and the struggles of immigrant communities. Yet, through it all, Vicky never lost her ability to find humor in the hardest of circumstances. It wasn't about diminishing the seriousness of these issues; rather, it was about finding moments of levity that could provide a sense of release in the face of adversity.

Vicky's humor became a way for her to connect with others, to break down barriers and build rapport with people from all walks of life. Whether she was interviewing a politician, a community leader, or a grieving mother, Vicky's ability to infuse humor into her interactions helped people open up and feel more comfortable. Her humor was disarming, a tool that allowed her to navigate difficult conversations while still keeping things light enough to avoid the heaviness that often accompanied the stories she told.

And it wasn't just her personal experiences that shaped her sense of humor. Vicky's role as a reporter allowed her to witness the humor of others—the comic relief that emerged from the most unlikely of places. She recalls spending time with families who had fled war-torn countries, laughing together over shared meals, even as they struggled to rebuild their lives. These moments of connection, in the face of hardship, became some of her most cherished memories.

One particularly poignant moment happened during a report she was doing on a family who had lost everything in a fire. As they recounted their story, the mother, a woman who had faced unimaginable loss, cracked a joke about how she was the only one in her family who hadn't yet learned to cook in the new kitchen. Her timing was impeccable, and the room erupted in laughter. In that moment, Vicky saw the power of humor—not as a way to erase pain, but as a way to navigate it. It was a reminder that even in the darkest moments, there was still room for light, for laughter, and for the human ability to find joy amidst suffering.

Vicky's ability to laugh through the tears became a hallmark of her personality—both in her personal life and in her work as a journalist. It wasn't just about being funny; it was about finding strength in vulnerability. Humor became a way for her to process the complexities of her identity—her experience as an immigrant, her journey as a woman of color in a predominantly white industry, and her ongoing battle with the trauma that came from her refugee past. Through humor, Vicky learned to embrace all parts of herself—flaws, insecurities, and all—and in doing so, she gave permission for others to do the same.

Humor in hardship, for Vicky, wasn't just a coping mechanism. It was an act of defiance—a refusal to be defined solely by the pain of her past. It was her way of saying, "Yes, I've been through a lot. But I am not broken. I am whole, and I will continue to laugh, even when it feels like I shouldn't." In many ways, her humor became the thread that connected her past to her present, her hardships to her triumphs. It was her way of showing the world that even in the face of adversity, there was still room for joy.

CHAPTER 10

FROM BOAT BABY TO BOSS LADY

Vicky Nguyen's journey from "boat baby" to a prominent national journalist and leader in the media industry is a remarkable testament to perseverance, grit, and the enduring power of mentorship and advocacy. Reflecting on the trajectory of her life and career, she sees not only her own transformation but the gradual shift in the media landscape that she's had a hand in shaping. Her story is one of breaking barriers, lifting others as she climbs, and pushing for a more inclusive, diverse, and representative industry.

It wasn't always a given that Vicky would end up as the powerhouse leader she is today. Like many first-generation immigrants, she had to balance the weight of expectations from her family with the pressure of carving out her place in a world that often seemed intent on making her choose between the two. As a child of Vietnamese refugees, Vicky's parents placed great emphasis on education, hoping it would be the key to a better life for her in America. But while her parents' dreams for her revolved around professional success, they also struggled with the cultural chasm that often separated their past in Vietnam from their present in the United States.

Early on, Vicky learned to juggle the complexities of identity. At home, she was the daughter of immigrant parents, absorbing their values and their trauma. But outside, she was often faced with the harsh reality of being "othered," of being too different to fit into the white-dominated spaces where she navigated school and later, the professional world. But through it all, Vicky's love for storytelling and journalism grew, and it became clear that her path was destined for more than simply finding a seat at the table—it was about creating a new table, one that was truly reflective of America's diversity.

When she first broke into journalism, it was with the understanding that the media landscape needed to evolve. In many ways, the field was—and still is—dominated by a narrow range of voices, stories, and perspectives. It wasn't that those voices weren't important, but the absence of others, particularly those from marginalized communities, was glaring. Vicky, with her unique background as a Vietnamese-American immigrant, understood that storytelling had to reflect the full spectrum of the human experience.

Breaking into the industry was not an easy feat. There were few role models who looked like her in the newsrooms she entered. Vicky had to prove herself time and again, not only to her colleagues but also to herself. The barriers were many: as an Asian-American woman in media, she faced implicit bias, challenges in being taken seriously, and often had to contend with the idea that her experience as a refugee and child of immigrants wasn't seen as "mainstream" enough for the stories she aspired to tell. Yet, with every challenge, Vicky became more resolute. Her passion for journalism was undeniable, and so was her belief in the power of diverse, representative storytelling.

One of the pivotal moments in Vicky's career was when she joined NBC News. It wasn't just a job—it was an opportunity to shape the conversation, to bring her own experiences and insights to the forefront. But even as her career soared, she didn't forget the road she had traveled to get there. Vicky knew that her visibility wasn't just for her own success; it was for the thousands of other young people—immigrant children, people of color, and those who had always felt underrepresented—who needed to see someone like them in positions of leadership. She often reflects on how, in those early days, she would have given anything to see a journalist like herself on the screen, someone who didn't just report the news but embodied it, someone who was connected to the very stories she was telling.

Vicky's ascent in the media world wasn't just about breaking barriers for herself—it was about lifting others along the way. She became an advocate for diversity and representation in journalism, not as an afterthought, but as an integral part of the industry's evolution. For her, the pursuit of diversity wasn't just about checking boxes or fulfilling quotas; it was about ensuring that stories reflected the lived experiences of a diverse nation. Representation, she believes, is not just about numbers—it's about giving voice to the voiceless, elevating the stories that have long been marginalized, and dismantling the structures that have historically silenced those who are different.

Her leadership, both on-screen and off, has always been centered on mentorship. Early in her career, Vicky was fortunate to have mentors who believed in her and helped guide her through the often murky waters of the media industry. She learned the importance of giving back, of providing that same guidance to the next generation of journalists who would follow in her footsteps. "When I got to the place I am today," she says, "I knew I didn't get here alone. And I promised myself I would never forget that." Her role as a mentor has not only shaped the careers of countless young journalists but has also helped diversify the faces and voices that appear on air, behind the camera, and in the editing rooms.

Vicky's commitment to diversity isn't just theoretical. She has fought for it on the ground level, advocating for programs that support journalists from underrepresented communities. She's been vocal about the need for newsrooms to create more opportunities for people of color, particularly women, to rise to leadership positions. It's not just about covering different stories—it's about having diverse decision-makers who can influence how those stories are told. Vicky sees the media as a reflection of society, and when society isn't reflected in the media, it perpetuates a cycle of exclusion and misrepresentation.

Her advocacy work has extended beyond just the newsroom. As a public figure, Vicky has used her platform to speak out about the importance of representation and the necessity of diverse voices in every facet of life—from politics to entertainment to business. Her personal story—of being a child of refugees, of navigating two cultures, and of overcoming immense odds to become a leader in her field—has become a source of inspiration for many who feel that their voices are not being heard. She doesn't just talk about diversity; she lives it, pushing for a more inclusive world by ensuring that those who have been overlooked finally get the recognition they deserve.

Perhaps one of the most powerful aspects of Vicky's leadership is her humility. Despite her accomplishments, she remains grounded in the values that shaped her: hard work, resilience, and the unshakable belief that everyone deserves a chance to succeed. Her story isn't one of individual triumph alone; it's about lifting up her community, her colleagues, and the next generation of journalists. She believes that true leadership isn't about being at the top—it's about making sure that the people around you are empowered to rise with you.

Reflecting on her journey from "boat baby" to "boss lady," Vicky sees the importance of representation in everything she does. She understands that it's not just about filling seats at the table; it's about making sure that the voices heard are diverse, authentic, and reflective of the world around us. In a media landscape that has often failed to live up to its promise of telling all stories, Vicky's leadership is a reminder that change is possible when we actively work toward it.

As she continues to break barriers, advocate for diversity, and mentor those who follow in her footsteps, Vicky Nguyen remains committed to the belief that her success isn't just for her—it's for all those who dream of a place in the media, in leadership, and in a world where every voice is heard.

CHAPTER 11

LESSONS FROM THE OCEAN

Vicky Nguyen often reflects on the journey that brought her to where she is today—one that began not in the comforting embrace of security, but in the uncertainty of an ocean crossing. As a child, she was but a "boat baby," one of many refugees escaping the chaos of Vietnam after the fall of Saigon, enduring a treacherous journey to a new life in a foreign land. Her story is a testament to resilience, to the strength that is forged through hardship, and the lessons that are learned in the midst of struggle.

The ocean, she says, taught her everything. It was vast and unpredictable, a reflection of the world she would soon encounter. In those early years, as she clung to the safety of her family and the hope of a new beginning, Vicky learned the profound truths about life that would guide her through the many challenges ahead. These lessons have not only shaped her into the journalist and leader she is today but also made her the person who is willing to share her story with others—to offer hope, perspective, and advice to those still navigating their own uncertain waters.

Strength: The Ability to Endure and Overcome

The journey across the ocean wasn't just a physical one; it was a test of endurance, an emotional and psychological ordeal that would prepare Vicky for every storm that would come in her life. It wasn't just the waves or the uncertainty of the journey that would challenge her—it was the knowledge that she and her family were leaving behind everything they had ever known. For Vicky, this was the beginning of understanding that true strength isn't always visible; sometimes, it's the quiet determination that you carry inside, the resolve to move forward even when the road ahead is unclear.

Growing up, Vicky's parents taught her that nothing worth having comes easily. They worked tirelessly to build a new life in America, often struggling to make ends meet. The lessons they imparted weren't always in words; they were in the actions of her mother, who worked multiple jobs, and her father, who silently bore the weight of sacrifice for his family's future. From their example, Vicky learned that strength isn't just about surviving—it's about thriving even in the most challenging circumstances. It's about getting up every day, doing the work, and believing that your efforts will eventually pay off.

This strength would become the foundation of Vicky's own journey in the media. In a field that often questioned her worth and visibility, she drew from that early experience on the ocean—an experience where the odds were stacked against her but survival was non-negotiable. She faced adversity in the newsroom, struggled to make her voice heard, and encountered the many biases that came with being a woman of color. But each obstacle was a reminder of the strength that had been passed down to her—strength that she knew, deep down, was a part of who she was.

Humility: The Importance of Staying Grounded

Despite the accolades, the awards, and the recognition she would eventually receive as a journalist, Vicky has always remained grounded. She credits this to the lessons of humility that were instilled in her from a young age. Her parents, in their quiet way, never sought recognition for their sacrifices. They didn't ask for gratitude—they simply did what was necessary to provide a better life for their children. Vicky learned that humility wasn't about diminishing your accomplishments but about understanding that no success is ever achieved in a vacuum. It's about recognizing the people who helped you along the way, the sacrifices made on your behalf, and the journey that brought you to this moment.

"I've always remembered where I came from," Vicky says, "and that has kept me grounded. I remember the struggle and how hard it was, and I never take for granted the opportunities I've had."

As Vicky's career took off, she often found herself in rooms with powerful individuals—news executives, media moguls, influential politicians—but she never let her success overshadow the values her family had taught her. She always remembered her roots, and as she rose in her career, she made it a point to lift others as well, especially those who didn't have the same access to opportunities. This humility is reflected not just in her professional life but in her personal relationships as well. Vicky credits much of her success to the support system of friends, family, and mentors who helped her along the way—and she never forgets the importance of giving back.

Faith: The Compass That Guided Her

Faith, for Vicky, was not just a religious belief, though that certainly played a role in her life. It was also a faith in herself, in her abilities, and in the larger universe that would guide her path. Faith, she believes, is the ability to trust that everything happens for a reason and that each challenge is a stepping stone toward something greater. Her faith was also rooted in the belief that her story—her family's journey—wasn't just about them. It was about the collective experience of refugees, immigrants, and marginalized communities.

"The ocean was a place of uncertainty," she says, "but it was also a place where I found my own faith in something bigger than myself. I realized that I wasn't alone—that there were people who cared, people who wanted me to succeed. That belief has carried me through everything."

Faith, she believes, is about being resilient in the face of adversity and having the conviction to keep going even when things seem impossible. Whether it was pursuing her dreams in journalism or standing up for diversity in the media, Vicky held on to the faith that she could make a difference. It was her guiding light when navigating both the personal and professional challenges she faced.

Gratitude: Recognizing the Gifts Along the Way

Gratitude is one of the central lessons Vicky learned from her family's journey—and it is a value she carries with her every day. She is grateful not only for the life she has been able to build in America but also for the struggles that came before. Her parents' sacrifices were not just burdens—they were gifts, lessons that shaped her and gave her the opportunity to reach heights they could only dream of.

"I don't take anything for granted," she says, her voice filled with sincerity. "I'm grateful for the struggle because it taught me what it means to work hard, to persevere, to appreciate every small victory. Gratitude grounds me, and it reminds me that my success is not just for me, but for my entire community."

Her gratitude extends beyond her own experiences to the larger immigrant community—those who still face hardships, those who are still working tirelessly to build a better future for their families. Vicky is adamant that we must never forget the sacrifices of the past, as they are the foundation upon which future generations can stand tall.

Advice for Immigrants and Children of Refugees

Looking back on her own journey, Vicky has words of advice for other immigrants and children of refugees who may feel lost or uncertain about their place in the world. First and foremost, she urges them to hold onto their story. The immigrant experience, the struggle, the triumphs—these are not burdens to be ashamed of but parts of a rich tapestry that will shape who they are. "You are not the sum of your struggles," she says. "You are the strength that you carry with you."

She also encourages them to never lose sight of their worth. The challenges may be many, but their voices matter, and they have the power to create change. In the media, in politics, in business—there is space for their stories. Vicky urges young immigrants and children of refugees to seek mentorship, to give back, and to lift others as they rise.

"The journey doesn't end when you arrive," she says. "It's just the beginning. You have the power to shape the world around you. Don't forget that."

The lessons learned from the ocean—the lessons of strength, humility, faith, and gratitude—have not only shaped Vicky's life but have allowed her to help others navigate their own seas. Her story is a beacon of hope for those still on the water, searching for a place to call home, and a reminder that the journey may be long, but it is always worth it.

CHAPTER 12

FULL CIRCLE – RETURNING TO VIETNAM

For Vicky Nguyen, the journey from Vietnam to the United States was one marked by hardship, sacrifice, and a profound sense of displacement. As a young child, she had been one of the many boat babies fleeing the fall of Saigon, seeking safety and a better life across a vast ocean. Decades later, as a journalist, Vicky had reached a level of success few could imagine when she and her family first arrived in America. Yet, despite the bright lights of her career and the accomplishments that came with it, there was an undeniable tug in her heart—a call back to the land of her birth, to the place where it all began.

Returning to Vietnam was never something Vicky had taken lightly. It was more than just a trip; it was a pilgrimage of sorts—a journey of healing, of reconciliation, and of coming to terms with the place she had been forced to leave as a young child. She had heard stories from her parents, tales of their struggle in the aftermath of the war, of their hopes for a brighter future, and of the overwhelming sadness they felt when they left behind the country they loved. But what she knew of Vietnam was only the one they had spoken about. It was a country in turmoil, a place full of pain and loss. And yet, it was also a place that had shaped who she was—a land whose culture, customs, and traditions still coursed through her veins, even though she had lived most of her life on foreign soil.

Her decision to return was not made on a whim. It was the culmination of years of reflection, of grappling with questions of identity, belonging, and the complexity of being both Vietnamese and American. For years, Vicky had built a life in the United States, carving out a space for herself in a media landscape that often overlooked or misrepresented her heritage. Yet, even with all that she had achieved, she felt a pull to understand her origins in a deeper, more personal way. Vietnam was a part of her, an integral part of her story, and it was time to face it.

The First Steps on Home Soil

When Vicky's plane touched down in Ho Chi Minh City, the weight of the moment hit her like a tidal wave. This was not just a place she had heard about in stories—it was the birthplace of her parents, the land they had fled, the soil that held the memories of a past that was both cherished and painful. She was in the country of her origin, but it was also a place that felt unfamiliar, foreign. The streets were crowded with motorbikes and bustling vendors, the air thick with the sounds and smells of a city alive with energy. But beneath the vibrant exterior, Vicky could feel the echoes of the past.

She visited the war memorials, places where the remnants of a divided nation still stood as reminders of a history she had never fully known. In Ho Chi Minh City, she saw the old French colonial architecture juxtaposed with the modern, growing metropolis. There were skyscrapers, luxury hotels, and high-end shops, but also narrow alleyways where families lived with little more than the bare necessities. The contrast between the old and the new was striking, but it was also a reflection of the internal conflict Vicky had long wrestled with.

For years, Vietnam had been a distant memory, a place that her parents tried to protect her from, sheltering her from the trauma they had experienced. Yet, as she walked through the streets, she began to feel the presence of her family's past in a way she had never imagined. There was a sense of deep loss, but there was also a sense of pride. The people around her, the ones who had endured so much, had rebuilt and thrived. Vietnam, too, had risen from the ashes.

Reconciliation with the Past

As Vicky traveled beyond Ho Chi Minh City to the countryside, she began to understand more about her parents' decision to leave, to start anew in a land that was as foreign to them as it had been to her. Her parents never talked much about their life in Vietnam, especially not about the war. But visiting the quiet villages and rural areas of the country, Vicky felt a deeper sense of connection to their experience. She saw the generations of people who had lived through the hardship and strife, people who had rebuilt their lives after so much devastation.

One particular trip took her to a small village where her parents had grown up. There, she met some of the older members of the community—people who had known her family, who had seen them grow up before the war. These were the people who had lived through the turmoil, who had felt the same fears and hopes that had fueled her parents' decision to flee.

The conversation was both heart-wrenching and healing. Vicky listened intently as they shared stories about her family—stories of laughter, of sorrow, of resilience. She learned more about her parents' childhoods, their dreams, and their struggles. It was an emotional reckoning. In many ways, this village felt like a place of both discovery and closure. It was here that Vicky finally understood the complexity of the decision to leave Vietnam, the deep love her parents had for their homeland, and the sacrifices they had made for the future they could only imagine.

Honoring Her Roots

Vicky's journey back to Vietnam was not just about reconciling with the past; it was also about honoring her roots. It was about recognizing the richness of her heritage and the resilience of the people who had fought so hard to preserve it. She spent time visiting cultural sites, tasting the foods she had grown up with, and reconnecting with the traditions her parents had passed down.

One of the most powerful moments came when she visited a small temple, nestled in the hills outside of Hanoi. The air was thick with incense, and the atmosphere was one of reverence. There, in the quiet of the temple, Vicky lit a candle for her parents—thanking them for their sacrifices, for their love, and for their strength. It was a moment of deep emotional release. The tears she had shed in the temple were not just for her parents but for the people who had suffered through the war, for the generations that had been lost, and for the future that had been built from the ashes.

Vicky also took the time to reflect on the way the Vietnamese diaspora had shaped her own identity. Growing up in the U.S., she had often felt torn between two worlds—the one of her parents and the one of her American life. In Vietnam, she came to realize that both worlds were part of her. She was not just a child of refugees; she was a child of Vietnam and America, a bridge between two cultures. Her journey back to Vietnam was not just a return to her roots; it was a reclaiming of her place in both worlds.

Healing and Moving Forward

Returning to Vietnam was a cathartic experience for Vicky. It allowed her to heal the wounds of the past, to understand her parents' sacrifices in a more intimate way, and to embrace the complexity of her identity. She realized that, while the war may have separated her family from their homeland, it had also made them stronger, more resilient.

The journey was not just about the past—it was about moving forward. Vicky returned to the United States with a renewed sense of purpose, with a deeper understanding of who she was and where she came from. Her return to Vietnam was a full-circle moment, a moment of healing, reconciliation, and honor. She had come to understand that, while the pain of the past would always be a part of her story, it was not the end of the story. There was still so much to be done, so many stories to tell, and so many people to lift up.

As Vicky looks back on her journey—from the boat to the newsroom to the streets of Vietnam—she knows that it is a journey that is never truly complete. It is a journey of discovery, of growth, and of honoring the past while embracing the future. And it is a journey that will continue to shape who she is, as she strives to make a difference in the world, carrying with her the lessons of the ocean and the wisdom of her ancestors.

Chapter 13

FULL CIRCLE – RETURNING TO VIETNAM

Vicky Nguyen's journey from refugee to national journalist has been one of determination, resilience, and, above all, a commitment to creating opportunities for others to thrive. As someone who had once been the child of immigrants, struggling to find her place in a foreign world, Vicky now found herself in a position of influence, able to tell stories that shaped perceptions and opened doors. But she never lost sight of her roots—the experiences of her family, the challenges of the immigrant community, and the power of storytelling to bring about change.

Now, in a career that has taken her to the forefront of national journalism, Vicky's focus has shifted toward building bridges for the next generation. She understood that the work wasn't just about her success but about uplifting others, especially those who shared her immigrant experience and faced the same barriers she had once encountered.

Her commitment to this cause went beyond merely reporting on issues; it extended to hands-on advocacy, mentorship, and active engagement in changing the narrative. Vicky's legacy wasn't just in her on-air appearances or her journalistic accolades—it was in the lives she touched, the stereotypes she helped dismantle, and the young voices she empowered to find their own place in the world.

Encouraging the Youth

One of the most impactful ways Vicky gives back is by reaching out to the youth. She is deeply committed to supporting young people who come from backgrounds similar to her own—immigrant families, communities of color, and those who have been overlooked by mainstream media. She frequently speaks at schools, universities, and community organizations, offering encouragement and advice to students who may feel as though they don't belong or who face significant obstacles in pursuing their dreams.

Growing up as a first-generation Vietnamese-American, Vicky had always felt the weight of expectation placed on her by her parents. They had come to America with nothing but hope and the desire to build a better life. They sacrificed so much, and their hopes were pinned on the possibility that their children could achieve what they never could. But that weight of expectation also came with the pressure of fitting in, of figuring out how to navigate a world where she was both too "foreign" to fully belong and yet not "American" enough to be accepted.

This duality—the feeling of straddling two worlds—was something Vicky knew many young immigrants struggled with. So, when she spoke to young audiences, she always tried to share her journey in a way that acknowledged those challenges. She often began her talks by telling them how she had been the first in her family to speak English, the first to go to college, and the first to navigate the world of journalism. But she also reminded them that she wasn't the last—that there were more opportunities than ever before, and that they, too, could find their voice and tell their stories.

"It's okay to be different," she'd say, smiling as she looked out over the sea of young faces. "It's okay to stand out. In fact, the world needs you to. Your story matters."

These words weren't just platitudes—they were grounded in her own experiences. She had learned early on that her identity as a Vietnamese-American was both her strength and her differentiator in the media industry. Her unique perspective allowed her to see the world through a lens that few others could—and that perspective was valuable, not a hindrance. It was something she wanted to impart to the next generation: to embrace their identities, to be proud of their cultures, and to use their experiences as a stepping stone toward success.

Fighting Stereotypes and Challenging Misconceptions

One of Vicky's greatest passions has been fighting stereotypes. As a journalist, she had witnessed firsthand how the media often misrepresented or oversimplified the immigrant experience. She knew all too well how easy it was for people to be pigeonholed based on their race or ethnicity, and she was determined to challenge those narratives.

In her role as a reporter and anchor, Vicky made it a point to cover stories that highlighted the complexity of immigrant lives. She sought out stories of success, resilience, and innovation within immigrant communities—stories that celebrated their contributions and showed their value beyond the stereotypes often associated with them. Whether it was reporting on the struggles of refugee families, highlighting the success stories of immigrant entrepreneurs, or delving into the challenges faced by second-generation Americans, Vicky used her platform to counter the oversimplified and harmful narratives that often dominated public discourse.

But it wasn't just about challenging the media; it was also about empowering those in her community to take control of their own stories. Through her work as a mentor and advocate, Vicky encouraged young people of color to become the storytellers of their own experiences, to fight against the narrative that said their voices didn't matter, or that they had to conform to some kind of ideal in order to be heard.

"I've been in rooms where I was the only one who looked like me," Vicky once shared in an interview. "And I know that feeling of being invisible. But here's the thing: your story has value, even when the world doesn't want to listen. You just have to keep telling it."

Her work—both on and off the screen—was always rooted in the belief that when marginalized voices are heard, society is enriched, and everyone benefits. She wanted to be a part of changing the landscape for future journalists, filmmakers, and creators of all kinds, encouraging them to break free from the mold and create new, authentic representations of the immigrant experience.

Celebrating Immigrant Stories

As much as Vicky worked to dismantle negative stereotypes, she also dedicated herself to celebrating the richness of immigrant stories. Her own story was testament to the fact that immigrants don't just survive—they thrive, they contribute, and they transform the places they call home. She believed that storytelling was a powerful tool for cultural preservation, and she saw it as an essential part of her mission to ensure that immigrant voices were celebrated, not erased.

She worked closely with organizations that focused on preserving the stories of the Vietnamese-American community, from oral history projects to media initiatives. Vicky saw these efforts as crucial in ensuring that the history and experiences of her people weren't lost to time. "Our stories are our legacy," she would often say, "and if we don't tell them, no one else will."

Her commitment to celebrating immigrant stories extended beyond the professional realm. She often hosted community events where immigrants could share their stories in a safe and welcoming environment. These events were not just about the exchange of personal histories—they were about fostering a sense of pride in one's heritage and contributing to the larger cultural mosaic of the United States.

Through these efforts, Vicky hoped to inspire future generations of immigrants to not just survive, but to thrive—to carve out a space where their experiences could be acknowledged, celebrated, and used to create positive change. She knew that the strength of any community lay in its ability to unite and share in its collective story, and she was determined to play a part in that unification.

Legacy in Motion

As Vicky continues to pave the way for young, diverse voices in the media and beyond, her legacy remains one of empowerment, advocacy, and unwavering commitment to making the world a better place for those who come after her. She understands that her success is not just about her—it's about the many others she's inspired and the doors she's opened for those who may not have otherwise had a chance.

Through her work, her mentoring, and her commitment to diversity, Vicky Nguyen is building a legacy in motion—a legacy that will continue to impact generations to come. And in the process, she is helping to ensure that the immigrant story, with all its complexities and richness, is told, understood, and celebrated by the world.

www.ingramcontent.com/pod-product-compliance
Lightning Source LLC
Chambersburg PA
CBHW022120090426
42743CB00008B/938